LIFE CYCLES

The Life Cycle of Insects

Revised Edition

Susan H. Gray

Chicago, Illinois

www.capstonepub.com
Visit our website to find out
more information about
Heinemann-Raintree books.

To order:
☎ Phone 800-747-4992
🖳 Visit www.capstonepub.com
to browse our catalog and order online.

© 2012, 2022 Heinemann Library
an imprint of Capstone Global Library, LLC
Chicago, Illinois

Edited by Abby Colich, Megan Cotugno, and Kate deVilliers
Designed by Victoria Allen
Illustrated by Darren Lingard
Picture research by Ruth Blair
Originated by Capstone Global Library, Ltd.

**Library of Congress Cataloging-in-Publication Data is
available on the Library of Congress website.**
  ISBN 9781484683187 (pb)
  ISBN 9781484683064 (ebook pdf)
  ISBN 9781484683132 (kindle)

Acknowledgments
The author and publisher are grateful to the following
for permission to reproduce copyright material: Alamy:
Avalon.red/Anthony Banniste, 13, Nigel Cattlin, 35, Ray
Wilson, 39; Getty Images: Bettmann, 7, Joe McDonald,
25, 32, Kevin Schafer, 11, Mike Powles, cover, Sir Francis
Canker Photography, 29, Valter Jacinto, 24; Minden Pictures:
Satoshi Kuribayashi, 27; Shutterstock: Alexey Stiop, 40, Alta
Oosthuizen, 28, Arsgera, 8, Bjoern Wylezich, 45, Charles
Shapiro, 22, Chris Mansfield, 12, Dhoxax, 19, ermess, 33,
Florian Andronache, 26, Foto Factory, 30, Geanina Bechea,
42, HTU, 23, Jan Miko, 31, Jubal Harshaw, 20, kzww, 37, Mark
Bridger, 14, Michael Pettigrew, 16, Mircea BEZERGHEANU,
4, petka, 17, Rob Hainer, 41, Subbotina Anna, 21, Szabolcs
Borbely, 38, vblinov, 15; SuperStock: Animals Animals/Carson
Baldwin JR, 10

We would like to thank Dr. Michael Bright for his invaluable
help in the preparation of this book.

Contents

Some words are shown in bold, **like this**. You can find out what they mean by looking in the glossary.

Look but don't touch: Many insects are easily hurt. If you see one in the wild, do not get too close to it. Look at it, but do not try to touch it!

What Is an Insect?

An insect is a small animal that has a hard body covering called an **exoskeleton**. Every insect has three main body parts—a head, a **thorax**, and an **abdomen**. The head has mouthparts, eyes, and a pair of **antennae**, or "feelers." The thorax has three pairs of legs and usually one or two pairs of wings. The abdomen contains organs for digesting food, for getting rid of wastes, for breathing, and for **reproduction**.

The damselfly lives near lakes and ponds. Here you can see the three main parts of this insect's body. The antennae and eyes are on the head. The wings are on the thorax. The abdomen is the last and longest of the three parts.

An enormous group

Insects are **invertebrates**. This means they do not have backbones. In fact, they have no bones at all. Insects are not the only invertebrates, though. Snails, worms, clams, shrimp, and crabs are also invertebrates.

Scientists have described about one million different **species**, or types, of insects. Some scientists believe that there may be millions more that have not yet been discovered. This should not be surprising. Every year, about 7,000 new insects are added to the list.

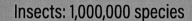

Insects: 1,000,000 species

Spiders: 40,000 species

Fish: 30,000 species

Birds: 10,000 species

Mammals: 5,000 species

The number of insect species far outnumbers the species of other animal groups.

What Are the Different Kinds of Insects?

Scientists have a huge job keeping track of all the different kinds of animals. Long ago, scientists realized they needed a way to organize them. They did this by creating many different animal groups, and sorting the animals into those groups.

First, scientists placed all animals into one enormous group called the animal kingdom. Then they divided the animal kingdom into major groups called **phyla**. Scientists took each phylum and divided it into groups called classes. They divided classes into orders, and divided orders into families.

Members of the same family are very similar to one another. However, they are different enough that scientists divide them into smaller groups called **genera**. Within each **genus** there may be one, or more than one, different **species**. Each species is one specific kind of animal.

Getting Organized

Carl von Linné was a Swedish scientist who lived in the 1700s. At that time, many new plant and animal species were being discovered. But scientists had poor methods for organizing them. They gave incredibly long Latin names to some of the plants. They grouped animals together based on where they lived. **Classification** was a mess.

Von Linné set up a system with orders, classes, and kingdoms. He grouped organisms according to their similarities. He gave every species a two-part Latin name. Von Linné got a little carried away with his system and even gave himself a two-part Latin name. Today, we know him as Carolus Linnaeus!

Carl Von Linné developed the classification systems we use today to keep track of living things.

Jointed legs

All insects belong to one huge phylum called Arthropoda. Arthropods all have legs with joints. The phylum of arthropods is divided into many different classes. There is a class for crabs and shrimp, a class just for centipedes, a class for spiders, a class for insects, and so on.

The class of insects has more species than any other arthropod group. Scientists divide this class into about 30 different orders. There is one order made up of butterflies and moths. Another order includes only the beetles. One order is for ants and wasps. And another consists only of termites.

Let's take a look at just one insect and figure out which groups it belongs to. This small insect is called the ladybug, or ladybird.

Here are a few of the groups in the animal kingdom. Where does the ladybug fit in? Which phylum, class, and order does it belong to?

Animal Kingdom
Phylum Porifera (sponges that live underwater and cannot travel)
Phylum Cnidaria (soft-bodied water animals including the jellyfish)
Phylum Platyhelminthes (flatworms with no legs)
Phylum Arthropoda (invertebrates with jointed legs)
Class Malacostraca (crabs and shrimp—the head and thorax are fused together)
Class Insecta (insects have a head, thorax, abdomen, and six legs)
Order Coleoptera (beetles, with two pairs of wings, one hard pair covering the other)
Order Lepidoptera (butterflies and moths)
Order Siphonaptera (fleas—wingless and have mouthparts built for sucking blood)
Order Odonata (dragonflies and damselflies—have long, slender abdomens)
Class Diplopoda (millipedes—arthropods with many segments and many legs)
Class Arachnida (spiders—arthropods with eight legs)

How Is an Insect Born?

All insects hatch from eggs. Mothers of different **species** lay eggs that differ in color, size, and shape. They lay either single eggs or clusters, on the ground, on the underside of leaves, on the sides of buildings, or other safe places. The tiny eggs seem to be delicate, but they are actually quite tough. Their outer coverings protect the developing insects and keep them from drying out.

Protect those eggs!

While all insects place their eggs in safe places, some put them in very unusual spots. They lay eggs on each other! The golden egg bug of Europe lays her eggs on males and other females. She glues up to 30 eggs onto their backs, legs, and heads. When the young hatch, they leave their carriers behind.

A Thoughtful Mom

After the female mud dauber wasp builds her tube-shaped nest, she begins hunting for spiders. Each time she finds one, she stings it to **paralyze** it, brings it back to the nest, and stuffs it into the tube. Later, she lays an egg in the tube and seals the hole. When the egg hatches, there's plenty of fresh, tasty food for the young.

This is an excellent survival trick. Several species of ants live in the same area as the golden egg bug. They all have a special taste for the bugs' eggs. But as long as something lugs those eggs from place to place,
the ants never have a chance to eat them.

Some wasps lay their eggs on or inside the bodies of caterpillars. When the young wasps hatch, they feed on the caterpillar's tissues.

Lots of eggs

Social insects are known for producing tremendous numbers of eggs. The social insects are those that live in **colonies**, sometimes with hundreds or thousands of individuals. Ants, bees, and termites are examples. In each colony, one female is responsible for laying all of the eggs. She is called the queen.

A new termite queen might lay only a few hundred eggs in her first year. However, an older queen can produce hundreds of thousands of eggs each year. She will tend her first batch of eggs. But worker termites will care for all later batches.

A few insects follow unusual **reproduction** patterns. Aphids are common insects that live on trees, bushes, and other plants. They lay eggs at one point in their lives and give birth to live young at another point.

When they are ready to hatch, the young become quite active inside the egg. Most species will chew or bite their way out. Baby fleas have a spine on their heads that they use to cut a slice in the egg.

Insects usually lay many eggs. But this does not mean that they will all hatch and grow up to be adults. Some eggs might dry out or become damaged in other ways. Of the young that do hatch, most are eaten by birds, fish, frogs, or other animals. Very few survive long enough to grow up and produce eggs of their own.

How Does an Insect Grow?

Among all of the insects, there are three basic patterns of growth (see pages 42–43). The most common pattern is the one that beetles, butterflies, and ants pass through. As they develop, they go through stages in which they have major changes in their appearance.

Time to split

After hatching from the egg, the new insect has a soft body and is very small and usually wormlike. This first stage is called a **larva**. Soon after leaving the egg, the larva's outer covering hardens. It is made of a material called chitin, and once it becomes hard, it cannot stretch. The larva will continue to grow, but becomes more and more tightly packed inside. In time, pressure builds up and the covering splits. The larva then crawls free, leaving the old covering behind. This process is called molting.

In time, the larva's outer covering hardens again, and the process repeats. With each molt, the larva grows a bit larger. During its young life, a larva might molt many times before entering the next stage of development.

Insects, such as this red lily beetle, molts many times before becoming an adult.

A Dangerous Time

While molting is necessary for an insect to grow, it is also dangerous. During a molt, the young insect cannot move freely. It may have part of its old covering stuck to its head or legs. It may have trouble squeezing through the split in the covering. Once it climbs free, the insect's body is soft and unprotected. It could become an easy snack for a bird or frog.

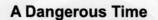

More changes

After a larva molts several times, it becomes a **pupa**. In this stage, the insect does not feed. In fact, it does not move about and it appears to be dead. However, many changes are taking place in its body.

Such major changes are especially evident in butterflies. In these insects, the larva is a caterpillar that feeds endlessly. It molts several times, allowing it to increase in size. In time, it stops eating and finds a safe place. The larva then spins a platform of silk, attaches its body to it, and dangles from it. The larva's outer covering splits and falls away one more time to reveal the pupa.

The silverfish develops differently from the butterfly and beetle. The young are tiny versions of their parents when they leave the egg. They do not pass through the larval stages, but still must go through molts in order to grow.

Some insects, such as this grasshopper, have their own method of development. At hatching, they look similar to the adults, but not exactly. With each molt, their bodies change only a bit, and they look a little more like an adult.

While it seems that the pupa is not alive, quite a bit is actually going on. In the pupa's body, the larval tissues are being destroyed, and the adult tissues are forming. This may take weeks or even months to happen. But when the time is right, the pupa's case begins to tear. Legs, **antennae**, eyes, and wrinkled wings poke through the split. Soon a fully formed adult butterfly struggles free.

How Do Insects Move?

Insects move and travel in just about every way imaginable. They crawl, run, burrow, leap, fly, swim, and skate (see page 31). Every insect has its own special muscles, wings, legs, and feet for its particular means of travel.

Insects have sense organs that give them information about their surroundings. These sense organs tell them when they are in danger and should flee. They also tell the insects when to move toward food or mates. The muscles and nerves in their legs and wings then help them to get going.

Antennae and eyes

On almost every insect's head is a pair of **antennae**. Insects use them to touch and smell their environments, or surroundings. Mosquitoes even pick up sounds with their antennae. Most insects also have eyes with many **facets**. These are called compound eyes. They can sense light, shadow, color, and movement, but do not see sharp images.

Even the tiniest insects have muscles and nerves that control their movements. When their antennae or eyes detect threats, their nerves immediately send chemicals to their muscles. The muscles respond by tensing and relaxing. When leg muscles do this, the insect runs or hops. When wing muscles tense and relax, the insect flies.

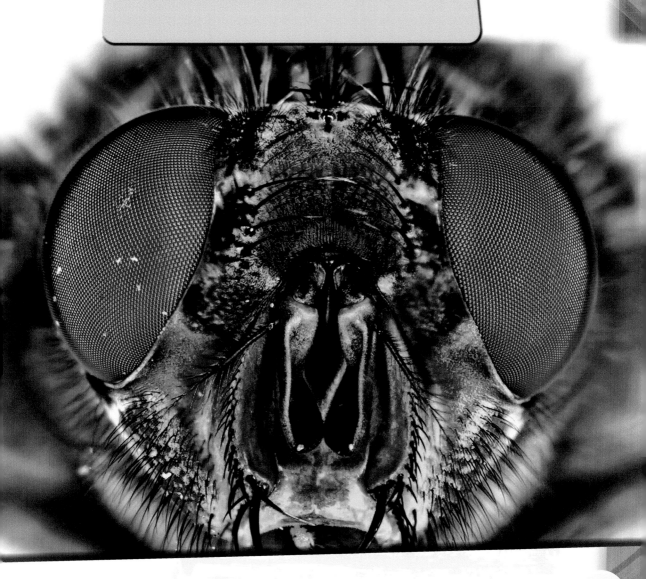

These compound eyes do not help the insect see clearly. But they are terrific at picking up changes in light, color, and movement. Some insects have compound eyes with only a few facets. But certain dragonflies have eyes with more than 25,000!

Some great legs

Insects are **arthropods**. The word arthropod comes from Latin words that mean "jointed feet." Arthropod legs have several joints. Thanks to these joints, insects can take small, delicate steps and they can make sudden tremendous leaps.

Water beetles are swimming insects. Their legs are flattened for paddling. Grasshoppers are outstanding jumpers. Their back legs are much longer than their other four legs. These back legs have two things that enable the insect to make its incredible leaps. Part of the leg contains large muscles. And at the "knee" there is a small organ made of stretchy fibers. This organ stores energy and releases it suddenly, sending the grasshopper into the air.

Mole crickets are burrowers. They dig burrows just beneath the surface of loose soil, looking for other insects to eat. Their front legs are large, broad, and shovel shaped—ideal for digging through the dirt.

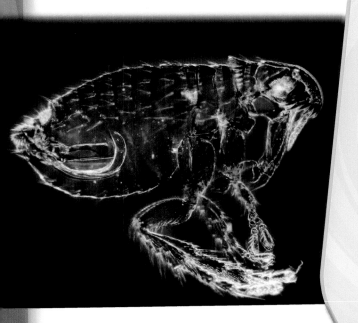

Whee!

A flea has two main ways to travel. It hitches rides on dogs, and it leaps amazing distances. While on a dog, the flea feeds on its blood. It can stay with the dog for days, traveling wherever the dog goes. But the tiny flea can also make a flying leap to another dog nearby. How? Fleas have little pads in their hind legs that contain an energy-packed substance. When the flea is ready to jump, the substance reacts explosively, sending the flea sailing.

Sticky tubes on the feet of the housefly help it walk along a wall or ceiling without falling off.

Flying

Most insects can fly. As adults, they have one or two pairs of wings. Most wings have a network of veins running through them. The veins carry a fluid called **hemolymph**. It acts as the "blood" of insects.

In insects with two pairs of wings, the pairs may not look at all alike. Beetles, for example, have a pair of hard, outer wings. These wings hide and protect the delicate pair of wings that do the flying. Houseflies also have two pairs. The front pair is large and easy to see. The back pair is tiny and club-shaped. They help to stabilize the insect as it flies.

Migrating monarch butterflies cluster together by the thousands each night.

Long trips

Most flying insects use their wings for short flights. Bees travel between flowers and their hives, and **cicadas** zip from tree to tree. But some insects make amazing cross-country trips called migrations.

In North America, monarch butterflies migrate from Canada and the northern United States. They travel to southern California and Mexico to escape the winter weather. At night, they cluster together to stay warm. At times, so many monarchs occupy the same tree that the branches break!

Bees not only walk and fly, but they also dance! Many scientists believe that after a bee discovers a new batch of flowers, it returns to the hive to tell the others. The bee does this by performing a dance. The dance movements tell other bees whether the flowers are nearby or far away, and which direction they are from the hive.

How Do Insects Protect Themselves?

When threatened, many insects actively defend themselves or their **colonies**. They bite, sting, or wrestle with invaders. Other insects defend themselves simply by hiding or sending warnings to their enemies.

Hiding insects might retreat into tunnels or underground nests. But some hide in plain sight. They do this by using **camouflage**. Their bodies blend in perfectly with their surroundings. The "leaf insects" have flat, green bodies. When they cling to a leafy branch, they are almost impossible to see. Insects called walking sticks use a similar trick. Their bodies are green or brown, and shaped like twigs. Some leaf and stick insects dangle from plants and rock back and forth. They look as if they are swaying in the breeze.

Hoverflies are insects that are completely harmless. They do not bite or sting. However, they look like wasps and bees. How might this protect them?

Warning! Warning!

Some insects use warning colors to scare their enemies. Bright red, orange, and yellow colors tell **predators** to stay away. Milkweed bugs, for example, are black and bright orange, and they taste terrible. A hungry bird might try one milkweed bug, but it will remember those bright colors before it tries a second one!

This caterpillar has bright colors that warn predators to stay away. But it also has something else. Those two big spots look like eyes, but they are not. Enemies might think the caterpillar is alert and watching them.

Look out!

For some insects, it's not enough to count on camouflage or warning colors. When these insects feel threatened, they go into action.

Sometimes ants invade termite nests. But at least one kind of termite is prepared for this. **Formosan** termites race toward the ants and begin pinching them. They work their sharp, curved mouthparts back and forth piercing the ants' bodies. If that doesn't work, the termites have another weapon. Thick, sticky liquid oozes from their heads. Some ants become trapped in the goo, while others manage to get away.

Female bees and wasps use their stingers to protect themselves and their homes. The stingers contain a small amount of **venom**. Honeybee stingers have backward-pointing hooks in them called barbs. These help the stinger to pierce the skin of an enemy. The wasp can draw its stinger out and use it again. But the honeybee's barbs get stuck. The stinger tears away from the bee and remains stuck in its enemy. This causes the death of the bee. To protect its hive, the bee sacrifices its own life.

This wasp can use its stinger to protect itself from enemies.

Bombs Away!

Bombardier beetles have wings, but many **species** are poor fliers or are slow to take off. When attacked, the beetle does not try to escape. Instead, it surprises its enemy with a boiling-hot bath. The beetle's body contains two separate packets of chemicals. When attacked, the chemicals mix and explode, causing hot, irritating fluid to spray from the beetle's body.

Where Do Insects Live?

Insects live underground, in trees, in swamps, and inside the lumber (wood) in houses. They live in the hottest deserts, the wettest rain forests, the most **remote** islands, and the highest mountains. Insects live just about everywhere.

They can do this because they are such terrific survivors. Their hard **exoskeletons** keep their bodies from losing water. This helps them to live in hot, dry areas. Most have wings, so they can easily escape danger. The tiniest insects can hide almost anywhere and the **camouflaged** insects can hide right out in the open.

This handsome grasshopper lives in the desert of the southwestern United States.

Building a unique home

Some insects, such as ants, bees, and termites, live in complex homes that they build themselves. Most people have seen anthills. Usually a hill is only a small part of the ants' home. Just beneath a hill is a system of underground tunnels with thousands of ants. One female is the queen. She is large, and she is the only ant in the **colony** to lay eggs. A few males live in the colony simply to mate with her.

Most of the ants are workers. These are females that cannot lay eggs. Instead, they take care of the queen's eggs. They also find food for the colony, build walls, dig tunnels, and defend the nest. The queen, males, and workers may look different and have different jobs, but they are all members of the same **species**. And working together, they help the entire colony to survive.

Some termites live secretly underground, but not the ones that built this mound. Termites of Africa and Australia create these amazing homes.

Life near the water

Some insects prefer to live near water. In fact, mayflies absolutely must live near the water. During the mating season, males and females fly together in thick swarms. They mate and the females lay their eggs. Some place their eggs on the surface of ponds, lakes, or rivers. The eggs sink and the young hatch underwater. The females of other mayfly species dive underwater and lay their eggs on plants or rocks.

One group of **aquatic** insects lives in a very unusual environment. These are the **intertidal** shore bugs. The intertidal area is along the seashore. During part of the day, the ocean rises to a point called high tide. Later, the water goes back down to a low point called low tide. The intertidal area is covered with water during high tide, but uncovered at low tide.

Amazingly, some shore bugs live here. During high tide, they hide in cracks between rocks. Scientists believe they breathe the air trapped there. During low tide, they rush out to eat food left there by the water.

Aquatic insects live along the shoreline. They find food during low tide.

Champion Skaters

These insects are called water striders or pond skaters, and they are built for aquatic life. Their middle and back legs are long and slender. These legs have hundreds of waterproof hairs. The legs and hairs lie flat on the surface of the water, allowing the insect to "skate" without sinking. The insect uses its back legs for steering. The middle legs propel (move) the insect forward. And the short front legs are for grabbing food.

How Do Insects Help Us?

Insects are helpful to plants and to other animals in many ways. They work as **decomposers** and help to improve the soil. When plants and animals die, insects decompose, or break down, their tissues. Beetles, ants, cockroaches, and termites move in and begin feeding on the dead matter. They digest it and form waste materials. These materials enrich the soil. Thanks to these decomposer insects, a rotting log becomes a place where new plants can grow.

The gardener's friends

Some insects are helpful to farmers and gardeners. They keep harmful insects from getting out of control. Praying mantises and ladybugs are just two examples. Mantises feed on leaf-eating insects and eat moths. The moths themselves are not harmful, but their **larvae** can destroy a garden overnight. Ladybugs eat aphids and other slow-moving garden pests.

Insects are an important food for many birds.

Bees are also helpful. They carry **pollen** between the blossoms of vegetable plants and fruit trees. This makes it possible for these plants to form seeds, vegetables, and fruits. Bees also produce honey, which is the favorite food of some animals.

Insects are not just helpful to soil and plants. They are also an important food for many birds, fish, frogs, and lizards.

A Valuable Worm

A silkworm is actually the larva of a type of moth. The larva spins a long silk thread, wrapping it around its body. This forms a case in which the insect spends its **pupal** stage. Silk farmers raise silkworms and patiently wait for them to become pupae. Then they carefully unroll the thread so they can sell it.

Troublesome insects

At times, insects have created big problems. Termites have ruined homes by eating the wood. And grasshoppers and **locusts** have destroyed crop plants by devouring their stems, leaves, and flowers. In some cases, this has happened after the insects came into new areas by accident.

How did the insects move there? Sometimes, insects become trapped in boxes that go onto cargo ships. They travel across the ocean and arrive in a new country. When people unload the ships and open the boxes, the insects are set free. Sometimes, they have no natural enemies in their new country. No other animals feed on them. When this happens, the insect population grows out of control.

This is what happened with an insect called the yellow crazy ant. It came to Australia from Africa or Asia in shipping crates. The ant eats crop plants, seeds, other insects, and even crabs. It feeds day and night. It is wiping out the food supply of many of the **native** species.

Mosquitoes

Some insects, such as the mosquito, spread disease. The mosquito can carry an organism that causes **malaria**, a disease that is common in Africa. An infected mosquito injects the organism into every person it bites. People with malaria have fever and chills and often die. Poisoning mosquitoes and draining the swamps where they live has helped to wipe out this disease in many places.

The aphid-like balsam woolly adelgid came to North America from Europe. It has since spread through many forests, where it kills fir trees by attacking their roots and stems.

How Do Insects Spend Their Time?

Insects, like other animals, have periods of rest and periods of activity. Insects cannot close their eyes. Scientists aren't sure when or how insects sleep. However, they do have times of the day when they seem to be resting.

Whether they are resting or active, insects are breathing. Like other animals, they need to take in oxygen. An insect does not breathe in through its mouth or a nose. Instead, air comes in through tiny openings ,called **spiracles**, in the **exoskeleton**. In some insects, the spiracles have flaps that open to let the air in. Once inside, air travels through a series of tubes. The tubes reach into every part of the insect's body, bringing oxygen to the tissues.

Here you can see the heart and main vessel running along the back of the insect. The spiracles are in a row along the insect's side. The breathing tubes run throughout the body.

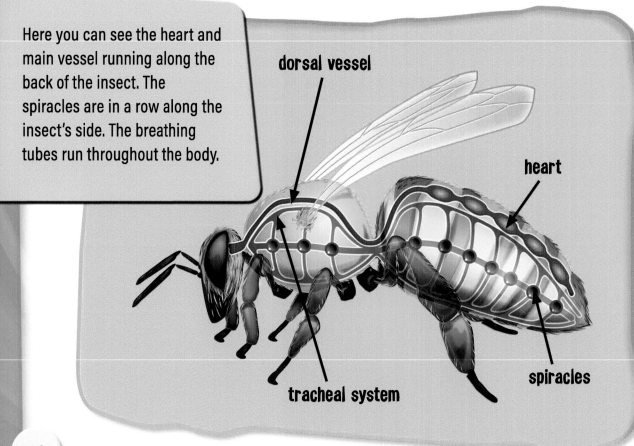

dorsal vessel

heart

spiracles

tracheal system

Like many other animals, insects have hearts. The insect heart is a multichambered tube in the **abdomen**, and it pumps **hemolymph**. When the tube squeezes, hemolymph moves through a vessel toward the head. When it reaches the head, hemolymph spills out of the vessel and washes over the insect's organs. It eventually moves back into the heart, to be pumped forward again.

Some insects make sounds by rubbing their legs or wings against their bodies. But not the Madagascar hissing cockroach. It forces air through its spiracles to make the hissing sound.

Insect meals

When insects are not resting, they are usually looking for food or eating. Insects have a digestive system that is a simple tube, starting with the mouth. Many insects feed only on plants. They are called **herbivores**. Some herbivores, such as grasshoppers, eat all parts of the plant—stems, flowers, leaves, and branches. Others prefer only the tender leaves of certain plants, or the nectar of flowers.

Insects that eat other animals, including other insects, are called **carnivores**. They are usually larger than their victims. They must trick or overpower their **prey** before eating it.

Decomposers are those insects that eat dead matter. The dung beetle is an unusual decomposer. It is attracted to the smell of animal wastes. The beetle forms the wastes into tiny balls. It then rolls the ball into a hole and lays an egg on it. When the egg hatches, the **larva** has the entire, delicious ball to feed on.

This dung beetle can decompose animal wastes.

Bug Spit

Many scientists today are studying the saliva of biting insects. They have found that the spit of the bloodsucking sandfly causes human blood vessels to widen. This brings more blood to the surface of the skin, so the flies can gorge on their bloody meal. If scientists learn exactly how the spit works, perhaps they can develop a drug to fight parasites carried by such insects.

How Do Insects Have Babies?

Before insects have babies, males and females must find each other and mate. Some insects use vision to spot their future mates. In butterflies, for example, the female's colors attract males. Other insects rely on light to find each other. The firefly is a beetle that flashes light from a special organ in its **abdomen**. In some **species**, only the males or the females flash. In other species, males and females flash signals to each other.

Not all firefly species can flash as adults. But all firefly **larvae** do. Some scientists believe this is how larvae protect themselves. The flashing tells **predators** to stay away.

Male horned beetles prove themselves to females by fighting the competition. They wrestle with other males, picking them up and throwing them on their sides. Moths use a much gentler approach. They can hear super-quiet sounds. A male will sing almost silently to females, hoping to find one that listens.

Not long after males and females mate, the female is ready to lay her eggs. Eggs are placed in safe places where the young insects will find plenty of food upon hatching. **Social insects**, such as hornets and wasps, build papery nests before the eggs are laid. Bees build waxy nests that can house thousands of eggs.

This moth quietly waits for a mate.

An endless cycle

Once the insects hatch, the life cycle continues. The young grow, molt, and repeat this pattern, growing larger every time. Once the insect becomes an adult, it is ready to find food, shelter, and a mate.

Some insects don't have a lot of time to mate. Mayflies spend only one or two days as adults. Their adult lives are so short that they do not even eat. They mate, lay eggs, and soon die. Other insects, such as ant and termite queens live for decades, producing thousands of young each year.

Most insects do not live long enough to have young. They die, or they are eaten by predators. But as long as some live long enough to produce eggs, the species will survive.

This mayfly will only live two days as an adult.

There are three basic life cycle patterns, although the egg to larva to pupa to adult pattern is the most familiar. These are:

Although their life cycles may be different, all insects go through changes from egg to adult.

• Egg to young (all look like small versions of the adult) to adult to pairing to eggs. The silverfish is an example of this life cycle.

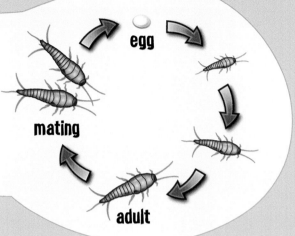

egg

mating

adult

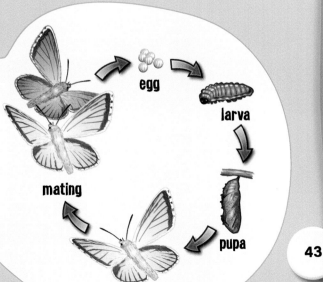

egg

nymph

nymph

nymph

mating

adult

• Egg to nymphs (gradually come to look like adults) to adult to pairing to eggs. Examples include crickets, termites, grasshoppers, and cockroaches.

• Egg to larva to pupa to adult to pairing to eggs (all stages look fairly different from one another). Examples of this life cycle are beetles, flies, lacewings, and butterflies.

egg

larva

pupa

mating

Insect Facts

What is the heaviest living insect?

The Goliath beetle of Africa weighs as much as a lemon. It is about 13 centimeters (5 inches) long.

What is the smallest living insect?

A tiny wasp called the fairyfly is the smallest insect known. Nearly 130 fairyflies in a row would equal 2.54 centimeters (1 inch).

What is the biggest insect that ever lived?

The biggest insect that scientists know about is the huge dragonfly called meganeura. It lived about 300 million years ago. Its wings measured 76 centimeters (30 inches) from tip to tip!

What is the loudest insect?

The **cicada** is the loudest insect. It can be heard 0.4 kilometer (0.25 mile) away.

Which insect lives the longest?

Termite queens are the winners here. They can live as long as 50 years.

Insect classification

Scientists place the million or so insects into about 30 different orders. The largest order by far includes the beetles—all 350,000 or so species. Smaller orders include the butterflies and moths, the dragonflies and damselflies, the grasshoppers and crickets, the stick and leaf insects, and the termites.

The **zorapterans** make up one of the smallest orders. These insects are only about 2.54 millimeters (0.1 inch) long and look like miniature termites. They form small colonies in rotting logs. Scientists know very little about them.

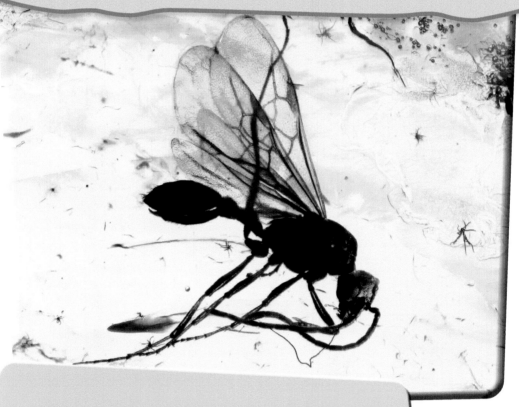

Millions of years ago, this insect became stuck in sap as it walked along a tree trunk. The sap hardened into what we now call amber. The ant was then preserved and never rotted away. Today, scientists can study such insects to learn what life was like on Earth long ago.

Glossary

abdomen last section of an insect's body

antenna (pl. antennae) sense organs on an insect's head that are used to feel objects and detect smells or chemicals

aquatic living in or near water, or dealing with water

arthropod invertebrate with jointed legs

bombardier type of beetle named for the person in a war plane who releases bombs

camouflage method of hiding by blending in with the surroundings

carnivore animal that feeds on the tissues of other animals

cicada large, flying insect

classification system for organizing things

colony group of insects living together

decomposer animal that breaks down the tissues of dead plants and animals

exoskeleton outer, hard covering of an arthropod

facet small, flat surface

Formosan having to do with the island of Formosa, now called Taiwan

genus (pl. genera) one of the classification levels of the animal kingdom

hemolymph fluid that circulates through an insect's body, bringing nutrients to the tissues

herbivore animal that eats plants

intertidal referring to the area along a shoreline that is covered with water during high tide, and uncovered during low tide

invertebrate animal without a backbone

larva (pl. larvae) young, undeveloped form of many insects

locust insect similar to a grasshopper

malaria disease that is carried by mosquitoes and may cause fever, chills, and even death

meganeura giant dragonfly that lived about 300 million years ago

migration trip made by animals, usually every year, to find food

native occurring naturally in an area

paralyze to make powerless or unable to move

phylum (pl. phyla) major groups within the animal kingdom

pollen powdery, yellow grains produced by flowers and necessary for producing seeds and new plants

predator animal that hunts and feeds on other animals

prey animals that are hunted and eaten by other animals

pupa (pl. pupae) one of the stages of development in some insects

remote far away

reproduction production of offspring

social insect insect that lives in a group

species particular kind of living thing

spiracle tiny opening along the sides of an insect for taking in air

thorax middle section of an insect's body, with legs and sometimes wings attached

venom poison

zorapteran member of one of the smallest insect orders

Find Out More

Books

Burns, Loree Griffin. *The Hive Detectives: Chronicle of a Honey Bee Catastrophe*. New York: Houghton Mifflin, 2010.

Markle, Sandra. *Termites: Hardworking Insect Families*. Minneapolis: Lerner, 2008.

Mound, Laurence. *Insect*. New York: DK Children, 2007.

Taylor, Barbara. *Science Kids Insects*. New York: Kingfisher, 2008.

Websites

National Geographic Kids: Creature Features
http://kids.nationalgeographic.com/kids/animals/creaturefeature

San Diego Zoo's Animal Byte: Insects and Spiders
www.sandiegozoo.org/animalbytes/a-insects.html

Smithsonian Institution: Entomology—BUGINFO
www.si.edu/Encyclopedia⊠SI/nmnh/buginfo/start.htm

Index